DISMANTLING DEMOCRACY

The forty-year attack on government,

...and the long game for the common good

BY DONALD COHEN

...

For Paul Booth, who challenged us all to think bigger,

act strategically and be in it for the long haul.

...

ISBN-13: 978-1533527264
ISBN-10: 1533527261

TABLE OF CONTENTS

INTRODUCTION

 Despite its legislative setbacks of the past year, the presidency of Donald Trump has been stunningly effective in its core mission, the dismantling of modern American government as it has evolved since the Progressive Era of the early 20th Century."

— SEAN WILENTZ,
Princeton University Historian [1]

After a year of the Trump administration, it's clear that the challenges we face are deep and long lasting. In the crudest and most heartless of ways, the election results are a significant milestone of the forty-year assault on government.

Beyond the specifics policies, actions and tweets, Trump's presidency has made clear that we are in values war. The conflict between unfettered individualism and the collective pursuit of the common good has endured in American culture and politics since the earliest days of the republic. But over the last forty-plus years, the assault on public solutions and the common good has reached unprecedented levels of intensity and sophistication.

The resulting challenges we face as a nation are profound:

1. **Unprecedented concentrations of wealth and power**

   a. Inequality in every (interconnected) dimension: economic, political, social, racial, and sexual

   b. Significantly increased private power over public goods that we all rely on for health, education, security, justice and community

2. **Fundamental changes in the economy**

   a. The shift from an industrial economy to a service economy, with an increasing share of activity in the financial sector

   b. An increase in the contingency of employment relationships, which has led to economic insecurity and underinvestment in occupational and professional development

3. Weakened institutional government capacity, making it more difficult to meet public needs

a. Massive disinvestment in social, economic, and physical public goods and assets

b. Increased privatization of public services and assets

c. Deregulation and lack of capacity to monitor and enforce basic health, safety, and other protections

4. Environmental catastrophe

a. Climate change threatens the planet as well as the social fabric of the country and world.

b. Persistent, and in some areas increasing, threats to public health.

5. Resurgence of the racism long embedded in American culture, economics, and politics

a. Increasingly bold and visible racist, homophobic, and anti-Muslim hate crimes, as well as police violence against young black men

b. Structural racism embedded in housing policy, employment, criminal justice, and education

6. Democracy at risk

a. Segregation and stratification that discourages the empathy and trust essential to public solutions and sacrifice

b. A coordinated assault on basic democratic rights: voter suppression, gerrymandering, and preemption of local authority

These conditions are both the result of and a driver of greater public distrust of, disdain toward, and disconnection from government that are now defining features of American politics, manifest in every election, every policy campaign, every public debate on the issues of the day.

It's critically important to recognize government is, and will always be, a work in progress, dependent on the values, interests and competence of those in power. Many who have held the reigns of government throughout American history have used policy and practice to institutionalize racism and exclusion. Despite many setbacks, we have both made progress and have far to go to remove those structural obstacles to full inclusion and equity. It's therefore understandable that African Americans, Native Americans, immigrants and others who have been denied full legal and legislative equality may be reluctant to put their trust in American government.

Unfortunately, if we believe in the common good, democratic governments are the essential institutions necesssary to ensure that our nation lives up to its values of shared prosperity, equality, and the protection of an interdependent planet. We need good government and transformed public institutions of all kinds that are responsive, effective and inclusive. They are the only way to solve many, if not all, of our common problems.

The attack on government has had consequences in virtually every area of public policy and public service: economic growth, economic security before and after retirement, taxation, affordable housing, health care, public health and safety, clean air and water, the social safety net, infrastructure, and on.

Progressives have won significant policy battles across the country in the past few years, such as minimum-wage increases and public investments in child care. But those victories have not translated into increased understanding of and support for the kind of basic public powers that they depended on. And the large-scale solutions we seek are simply beyond our reach without broad support for public action to advance the common good.

The bottom line is that progressives are losing the larger war for the soul of the nation.

The bottom line is that progressives are losing the larger war for the soul of the nation. Negative attitudes toward government and the dominance of free-market ideology have created a political environment that allows conservatives to sustain an agenda of austerity, privatization, and deregulation.

How Did We Get Here?

It wasn't always this way. While certainly not complete nor perfect, there were many significant legislative and regulatory victories during the 20th century that reflected strong support for government action. Today, drugs and food are safer than they were 100 years ago, Social Security and Medicare lifted millions of seniors out of poverty, our air is cleaner than it was during the 1960s and 70s before the Clean Air Act passed, asbestos, lead and other carcinogens have been removed from buildings and products and many other important actions.

But since the 1970s a constellation of aligned conservative institutions, grassroots issue groups, academics, intellectuals, industry leaders, and politicians has been enormously successful at shifting fundamental attitudes toward government and its basic role in American society. These groups have focused on winning the hearts and minds of the people not with detailed policy prescriptions but with a set of beliefs and conventional wisdom, a vaguely defined national philosophy that protects the privileges of the wealthy and powerful.

...

 *The Right may have looked formidable, but the reality is that it was a mess —
a contentious collection of disparate, often contradictory ideas and
querulous and warring factions of libertarians, chamber of commerce types,
traditionalists and social conservatives."* [2]

— **CHARLIE SYKES**, author of *How the Right Lost Its Mind*

...

These loosely affiliated groups weren't operating from a master plan. To describe
their efforts as coordinated, unified, or controlled top-down would be misleading.
Conservative foundations helped create a think-tank infrastructure in the 1970s and
1980s, with considerable overlap of funders and ideas. But over the same period,
a larger, more diverse array of conservative political, social, and economic forces [3]
became increasingly aligned. And they effectively rode waves of discontent created by
the Vietnam War, Watergate, and post-Vietnam economic problems.

The ideological and economic forces that have driven the assault on government
could be categorized as follows:

- ▶ **True Believers.** Free-market liberal ideologues (of various stripes) aim to
  fundamentally redefine our relationship with government, so that instead
  of being citizens with right and responsibilities, we become individual
  consumers of public services, a scenario in which we get only what we can
  pay for. That's a market society, not a democratic society. [4]

- ▶ **Self-Interested Ideologues.** "Corporate libertarians" such as the Koch
  Brothers [5] see themselves as warriors for free-market ideas — ideas that also
  conveniently serve their personal interests. They earn more money and gain
  more power by reduced regulations, lower taxes, and fewer unions. They
  are antigovernment in every respect, except when they can somehow benefit
  from the $7 trillion in annual government spending or from regulations
  that support their specific interests in competitive markets.

- ▶ **The Political Class.** The careers of conservative politicians depend on the
  successful implementation of their agenda to deregulate, privatize, and
  hobble political opponents, such as unions and voter-registration groups.

▶ **Social Conservatives.** Religious forces envision themselves as shock troops for individual freedom and for the dominance of religious law over civil law. They resent any government rule that they consider in violation of their faith. They were ripe for recruitment to the ideological antigovernment movement after Roe v. Wade. Similarly, the NRA over the last four decades has created a powerful and effective political base militantly committed to protecting the freedoms they believe are enshrouded in the Second Amendment.

Despite momentary backlashes that punished the party in power, these forces have successfully shifted American attitudes toward government and public solutions to the right. In 1958, a whopping 73 percent of Americans said they had faith in the federal government; in 2015, public trust in government was just 19 percent— a historic low.

Public Trust in Government Near Historic Lows
% who trust the government in Washington always or most of the time

Source: Pew Research Center[6]

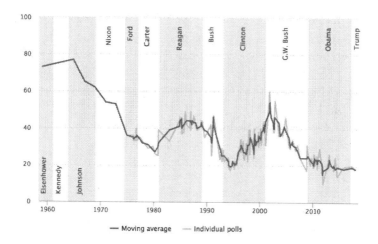

Though it wasn't a united project, it added up to a multifaceted strategy to accomplish a simple objective: to convince the American public that government is "the problem" in hopes of shrinking it, reducing regulatory and tax burdens, and capturing control of public resources. They are using that success to implement a conservative governing and economic agenda, tilting the benefits of government toward private interests and shifting fundamental shared responsibilities to the individual.

The Critical Element: The Corporate Counterattack

In the wake of the new consumer, auto, worker, and environmental safety laws of the 1960s and early 1970s, corporate America thought deeply about how to make the country more "business-friendly." Recent analyses focus on the development of a conservative infrastructure since Lewis Powell's infamous 1971 memo to the U.S. Chamber of Commerce, which served as a clarion call to defend capitalism against the likes of Ralph Nader, Rachel Carson, and liberal academics. Several important books have recently been published describing this history of pro-corporate conservatism in the United States (see bibliography).

Business interests have successfully used public distrust of government and their growing power to create policy and law that has restructured society to their benefit.

There were other efforts, in addition to the Powell memo, that helped unify the business community in this period. For example, in 1974 and 1975 the Conference Board, a business organization of major corporations, held six three-day strategy sessions with corporate leaders[7] to grapple with the large issues facing businesses in this new political context. These efforts led to several key insights:

▶ Business actors needed to function as a coordinated group rather than as separate industries focused on narrow interests.

▶ Individual companies with "brand sensitivity" needed to step back and hide behind groups such as the Chamber of Commerce, the National Federation of Independent Business (NFIB), and issue-specific "front groups" (many created by Rick Berman) to avoid consumer backlash.

▶ The business community needed to invest far more in politics and lobbying and build an infrastructure of think tanks to engage in the "battle of ideas."

Later, conservative strategists like Richard Viguerie and Paul Weyrich added significant political strategies to the mix that helped build conservative mass bases and realigned traditionally Democratic constituencies.

As a result of these insights, many institutions and individual actors began to pursue a set of overlapping, increasingly aligned, well-resourced efforts; these efforts developed their own momentum and began reshaping the political and economic landscape.

Business interests have successfully used public distrust of government and their growing power to create policy and law that has restructured society to their benefit.

For example:

▶ The tax burden has shifted from corporations and the wealthy to individuals and the middle class and led to cuts in public services—which then furthers popular discontent with public institutions.

▶ Attacks on government, accompanied by exalting the supposed efficiency of the private-sector, have opened the door to increased privatization of public goods and assets.

▶ Regulatory policy has been slowed down by requiring considerations of projected (and often exaggerated) costs over benefits, thereby enshrining the notion that the cost of a new regulation could outweigh the dollar value of the health, safety, and security of a child, working adult, or elderly parent.

▶ And judicial appointments have made it easier for conservatives to use the legal system to limit democratic rights and collective action to address significant problems.

> The weakening of both the *idea* of public solutions and the *institutions* of government has created major and, in some cases, seemingly impenetrable obstacles to solving many of today's problems.

The election of Donald Trump and recent fractures in the Republican Party are shaking up the coherence and alignment of conservative forces. But these differences are not dislodging fundamental attitudes towards government nor support for the fundamentals of conservative economics among them.

There's More at Stake than You Think

More troubling than the lack of faith in government institutions is the significantly weakened commitment to a notion of the *public itself*, built on mutual connection and the collective pursuit of the common good. The individualist pursuit of security and success in what economist Jared Bernstein calls a YOYO (you're on your own) world has overtaken the WITT (we're in it together) world of shared sacrifice, shared responsibility, and broadly shared benefits.[8]

If we are on our own and our connection to government is solely through the specific services we "consume," then we may fail to see and feel the commitment to pay for the services—like education—that others use. From this perspective we might ask why men should pay for health insurance that includes prenatal and maternity care when they will never give birth to a child. A congressman recently argued that we should "get rid of some of these crazy regulations that Obamacare puts on [...] such as a 62-year-old male having to have pregnancy insurance."[9] Racialized dog whistles continue to be used to divide the "deserving" from the "underserving" that further weakens the ties between us.

The weakening of both the *idea* of public solutions and the *institutions* of government has created major and, in some cases, seemingly impenetrable obstacles to solving many of today's problems. Without effective and efficient government that vigorously advances the public interest, we are powerless to tame the excesses of a capitalism that leaves too many in poverty; pollutes our water, air, and workplaces; and erodes the economic security of our families and the nation.

Why this Booklet?

Much has been written about the institutions, funders, and vehicles of the conservative infrastructure. Far less has been written about *how* this developing infrastructure (think tanks, media outlets, front groups, 527s, and PACs) has gone about shifting the nation's ideological ecosystem, changed popular beliefs, and established new conventional wisdom about governments and markets.

Over the past several decades, progressives have gone through periods of focus on particular aspects of conservative action, such as institution-building, message-development, and movement discipline. There wasn't one strategy or one secret plan but rather multiple strands, sometimes parallel and sometimes in competition, that in concert have amounted to an effective attack on government.

Part I of the paper is an attempt at an analysis of these strategic directions in order to expose their essential elements. It is meant to provide an overview; as such, it necessarily gives short shrift to complex dynamics and factors, perhaps leaving out important actions and players entirely. Instead, it is intended to identify the key pieces of a multisided strategy. It tackles the big picture, at the 30,000-foot level.

Part II is an attempt at ideas and strategic paths for the long haul. It lays out ten potential strategies to build a movement and a nation rooted in protecting and advancing the common good.

Any discussion of strategy should be as dynamic as the world around us; there have been and will continue to be new developments, new players, unexpected turns of events. This booklet does not lay out the one right answer. And it doesn't pretend to be conclusive, comprehensive or even right but rather aims to stimulate ongoing reflection, dialogue, and debate among the broad and diverse progressive infrastructure. This booklet is decidedly *not* about the next election. It is also not about policy or specific elements of a progressive agenda. It is simply a plea for serious inquiry, discussion and debate about the long term — where we want to go and how to get there.

Finally, a note of warning: don't read Part One without reading Part Two. The analysis will be incomplete, and you'll get the wrong impression that things are hopeless. They are hard, but definitely not hopeless.

...

" *Over the past three decades, we have drifted from having a market economy to becoming a market society."*

— **MICHAEL SANDEL,**
Harvard University.
Author of "What Money Can't Buy:
The Moral Limits of Markets."

...

PART 1 THE STRATEGIC ELEMENTS OF THE WAR ON GOVERNMENT

   " *As the experience of the socialist and totalitarian states demonstrates,*

the contraction and denial of economic freedom is followed inevitably by

governmental restrictions on other cherished rights. It is this message, above

all others, that must be carried home to the American people."

— **LEWIS POWELL**,
Memo to U.S. Chamber of Commerce, 1971

Over the past four decades, conservative forces have carried out a set of interdependent, if uncoordinated, strategies in order to discredit government and secure political control over public goods. Based on extensive readings and engagement in dozens of issues and political campaigns, five key strategies emerge along with their implementing tactics. Other elements may well be at play, and doubtless the material could be presented differently. Anything that attempts to paint a comprehensive picture could either fall of its own weight or be too simplistic to be useful. I'll let the reader judge, disagree, or add depth.

1. Engage in a War of Ideas: Freedom for Whom?

The post-WWII era was a tough time for conservative economists, academics, intellectuals, and business leaders. Social Security, the Tennessee Valley Authority, the Securities and Exchange Act, and other New Deal programs seemed to them a dangerous expansion of government's role in the economy and society—nothing short of a frontal assault on freedom and the beginnings of socialism in the United States.

The basic ideological contest in this country has always been a battle over the definition of freedom. It remains the core issue that defines competing worldviews today. The 20th-century New Deal consensus is based, in large part, on FDR's belief, which he shared with Congress, that "true individual freedom cannot exist without economic security and independence."[10]

FDR's Four Freedoms

On January 6, 1941, President Franklin Delano Roosevelt gave his famous Four Freedoms speech.[11] The following are excerpts.

FREEDOM OF SPEECH
FREEDOM OF WORSHIP
FREEDOM FROM WANT
FREEDOM FROM FEAR

The basic things expected by our people of their political and economic systems are simple. They are:

▶ *Equality of opportunity for youth and for others.*

▶ *Jobs for those who can work.*

▶ *Security for those who need it.*

▶ *The ending of special privilege for the few.*

▶ *The preservation of civil liberties for all.*

▶ *The enjoyment of the fruits of scientific progress in a wider and constantly rising standard of living.*

[W]e look forward to a world founded upon four essential human freedoms.

▶ *The first is freedom of speech and expression.*

▶ *The second is freedom of every person to worship God in his own way.*

▶ *The third is freedom from want, which, translated into world terms, means economic understandings which will secure to every nation a healthy peacetime life for its inhabitants — everywhere in the world.*

▶ *The fourth is freedom from fear, which, translated into world terms, means a world-wide reduction of armaments to such a point and in such a thorough fashion that no nation will be in a position to commit an act of physical aggression against any neighbor — anywhere in the world.*

Conservatives, on the other hand, have successfully embraced and captured both the language and the idea of freedom as rooted in individual choice, even while their definition of "individual" includes corporations.[12]

Killing Keynes: From the Four Freedoms to Free to Choose

Free-market theorists have long focused on dismantling the post-WWII "Keynesian consensus" that was the basis for popular support of the welfare state and government action to address market failure. The ideas of economist John Maynard Keynes so dominated the post-New Deal period that even Richard Nixon proclaimed, "We are all Keynesians."

Economist John Kenneth Galbraith's less popular but still influential idea that countervailing powers (government and unions balancing private industry) create shared prosperity needed to be replaced by individual choice and market competition as the key drivers of economic growth and prosperity.

The first step had to be discrediting the popular idea of government's positive role in the economy and then to substitute an alternative intellectual framework that established the

Paul Ryan ✓
@PRyan

Follow ∨

Freedom is the ability to buy what you want to fit what you need. Obamacare is Washington telling you what to buy regardless of your needs.

12:38 PM - 21 Feb 2017

"market" as the legitimate instrument of freedom and government as the obstacle to progress. The free market, they say, as the expression of individual choices is, in fact, the most democratic of institutions and that the "natural laws" of supply and demand, are more capable of delivering economic growth and shared prosperity. By this logic the population's individual consumer choices—not the democratic act of voting—lead to the best, most democratic outcomes for society.

Public Choice Theory, advanced by Nobel Prize economist James Buchanan[13] and other conservative economists, became the conservative intellectual response to the idea of market failure by positing equally dangerous "government failure." Government, the theory asserts, is inherently incapable of meeting people's needs because government bureaucrats and special interests manipulate the political process for their own ends. And where markets fail, government interference in markets will only make things even worse.

In the post-WWII years, a set of thinkers and economists built an intellectual body of work that articulated the superiority of markets and the ineffectiveness of government in creating prosperity; it asserted that incentives, competition, and choice drive innovation and government action stifles progress. Major voices promoting this perspective included Milton Friedman, Jude Wanniski, George Gilder, James M. Buchanan, and, of course, Ayn Rand. They debated, published books and seminal articles, and even hosted TV series that developed, described, and promoted a different view of American freedom.

Austrian-born economist Friedrich von Hayek was one of the movement's early intellectual leaders. His 1944 book *The Road to Serfdom* was met with surprising success, with excerpts printed in *Reader's Digest* and *Look* magazine. Considered the wellspring of antigovernment, pro-market ideas, the book continues to have a considerable influence on politicians, journalists, and business leaders. House Speaker Paul Ryan considers Hayek his intellectual guru.[14]

Public support for government remained high throughout the postwar years as public services expanded and the economy grew. The first signs of hope for conservative intellectuals came in 1962, with the publication of Milton Friedman's *Capitalism and Freedom*.

Yet despite the book's success, public support for government remained high throughout the postwar years as public services expanded and the economy grew. As a result, Hayek and his colleagues at the Mont Pelerin Society, a group of free market intellectuals created by Hayek,[15] were powerless to stem the continued growth of government activities throughout the 1950s and early 1960s. The first signs of hope for conservative intellectuals came in 1962, with the publication of Milton Friedman's *Capitalism and Freedom*. Friedman was an effective promoter of two critical ideas: governments were just like markets, and government was a public monopoly. Both of these became central arguments for privatization advocates in the 1970s and '80s.

Friedman's 1979 book, *Free to Choose*,[16] written with his wife Rose Friedman, became a guiding force in the governing philosophy of President Ronald Reagan. The book was a frontal assault on a "painfully collectivized world" and the welfare state. From there it was a short rhetorical leap to the oft-repeated Reagan remark, "The nine most terrifying words in the English language are 'I'm from the government and I'm here to help.'"

Notably, the most influential books, those with the broadest reach and largest number of acolytes, including Paul Ryan, Alan Greenspan, and millions more, were not written by economists but rather works of fiction by the novelist Ayn Rand. *The Fountainhead* and *Atlas Shrugged* describe the horrors of a dystopian totalitarian collectivism (a.k.a. the welfare state); in this world where "I" has been replaced with "we," the only viable opposition is radical libertarianism, motivated by extreme individual self-interest.

By the 1980s, this ideology began to dominate elite discourse, and supply-side economics became the populist—yet utterly false—economic theory that served as the ultimate antidote to a Keynesian management of the economy. This political program unleashed a massive shift in power and wealth in the United States.

By the end of the 1990s, Alan Greenspan's tenure at the Federal Reserve Board had further elevated the market as the dominant social metaphor, one that described not just economics but society itself. In the words of Harvard philosopher Michael Sandel, "Over the past three decades, we have drifted from having a market economy to becoming a market society."[17] Citizens had become consumers—of private goods and public services.

The Rediscovery of the Market:
Shifting the Dominant Policy Paradigm from Citizen to Consumer

The 1960s and early 1970s saw regulatory successes that made automobiles and workplaces safer and the environment cleaner; these included the Clean Air Act, the Occupational Safety and Health Administration (OSHA), and the Environmental Protection Agency (EPA). In response, business leaders and conservatives raised alarms. They developed a strategy to shift the dominant lens through which policy debates took place, from one focused on health and safety to one based on economics and costs.

When Ronald Reagan assumed the presidency, the front-line attack on the regulatory role of government became about the inflated costs (and job losses) resulting from existing and proposed regulations. Policy and procedural changes were set in motion requiring cost-benefits analyses, creating additional complexity for the approval of new regulations, and expanding congressional and executive-branch involvement in the regulatory process.

In the legal realm, an obscure 1960 journal article entitled "The Problem of Social Cost," by British economist Ronald Coase, ushered in a paradigm shift that infused market models into law. For Coase, everything had a price tag. The Coase theorem, as it became known, established that social good could be defined as a market-maximization problem that would be arbitrated by private-market actions. The Law and Economics Movement, launched by this theorem, attracted the support of conservative foundations, which invested in academia with endowed chairs for conservative scholars at law schools and schools of economics.

And, importantly, economists became increasingly embedded in schools of education, public policy, and other academic disciplines to the extent that market thinking began to influence those other fields.

Because of these efforts, the ideas eventually became mainstream. The future Supreme Court justice Steven Breyer wrote in the early 1980s that this "body of economic principles…offers objectivity—terra firma—upon which we can base decisions."

Creating the Ideological Army

The much-discussed Powell Memo,[18] by Chamber of Commerce attorney and future Supreme Court Justice Lewis Powell, issued a clarion call for sustained corporate investment in developing conservative academic institutions. These centers would challenge leftist control of universities and become a font of pro-market ideas. As has been written about by many scholars, the creation and success of these hubs at the University of Chicago and George Mason University, among other places, shifted scholarship to the right and produced a growing cadre of conservative intellectuals who would serve the cause.

The Koch Brothers are at the center of the current effort to influence universities and recruit 'free-market' scholars.

The Koch Brothers are at the center of the current effort to influence universities and recruit 'free-market' scholars. They have given millions of dollars to support free market economics programs at hundreds of universities and colleges since the 1970s. They have significantly ramped up their giving in recent years. In 2012 the Koch foundations distributed $12.7 million among 163 college campuses in 41 states and the District of Columbia during 2012.[19] By 2016, that amount had risen to $44 million.[20]

2. Turn Ideas into Conventional Wisdom: A 40-Year Narrative Success Story

To have impact, ideas must become widespread conventional wisdom, popular beliefs about human nature and how the world works. Only the transformation of ideas into beliefs—not economic analysis or policy issues—makes for enduring shifts in public attitudes and voting patterns. Success in creating conventional wisdom, what some call "cultural common sense", establishes the boundaries of the possible in policy action.

In her book *The Samaritan's Dilemma*, Dartmouth professor Deborah Stone emphasizes the significance of the public philosophy and ideas that undergird a political movement:

> *Public philosophy is the deepest form of political power. It's more potent than having the votes to pass a bill in Congress and more potent even than having the clout to prevent a bill from coming up for a vote. It's more potent because it's invisible, because no one official or even group holds it, and because it influences the way we think without us ever noticing a jolt to the brain.*[21]

How the World Works: Creating Conventional Wisdom about Government and Markets

The conservative assault on government has successfully embedded the following basic beliefs about government and markets in the world view of large segments of the American electorate. For many people they have become the default understanding of how the world works. We confront them every day, in every effort to advance a progressive agenda:

▶ Government is inefficient, bureaucratic, and wasteful. And most (all?) politicians are corrupt.

▶ Government serves someone else, not you. In the 1980s it was "welfare queens," or Medicaid and food-stamp recipients (i.e., the undeserving poor and demographic segments that the image evokes—people of color). Today it's politicians, government bureaucrats, and public-sector unions. Interestingly, many conservatives also believe that government serves the powerful (i.e., Wall Street, corporations), a view many progressives share, but this belief only increases their disdain for and distrust of government (and all large institutions.)

▶ Regulation and taxes hurt the economy, threaten your job and your freedom, and increase prices for the things we all need.

▶ The private sector is more efficient than government.

▶ America's real heroes are individual entrepreneurs, who are the engines of economic growth, while public workers are lazy and incompetent.

There are probably others we can think of that have seeped into DNA of American culture and politics.

It's important to recognize that these ideas and themes resonate with broad cross sections of the public— far beyond conservative voters. For example, competition, a key pillar of neoliberal and conservative ideology, can also be an important and positive force in the economy to protect consumers and small business and drive innovation. Conservatives recognize that competition is embedded deeply within our cultural and personal DNA, reinforced in many aspects of our lives – including commerce, sports, war, politics, art and more. Unfortunately, they have captured the language and ideology of competition to elevate markets over public solutions. Our challenge is to show that competition without rules can also work against the common good and weaken democracy, create a race to the bottom, increase inequality and harm important public goods like public education and a healthy environment.

We have seen many times how these basic beliefs often define the boundaries of the possible. It is difficult to raise new public revenues when citizens believe that the government already has enough money but simply wastes it. It's easy to advance a proposal to privatize public services if people believe that competition forces private enterprises to be inherently more efficient. The list goes on.

Not Just Dog Whistles:
It's about Race

As has been clear to many of us for a long time, race has been used to drive wedges in the American electorate. We even have a smoking gun. In 1994, John Ehrlichman, former advisor to Richard Nixon and convicted felon, was interviewed about the drug war. His response needs no elaboration:

❝ *You want to know what this was really all about? The Nixon campaign in 1968, and the Nixon White House after that, had two enemies: the antiwar left and black people. You understand what I'm saying? We knew we couldn't* *make it illegal to be either against the war or black, but by getting the public to associate the hippies with marijuana and blacks with heroin, and then criminalizing both heavily, we could disrupt those communities. We could arrest their leaders, raid their homes, break up their meetings, and vilify them night after night on the evening news. Did we know we were lying about the drugs? Of course we did."* [22]

Kevin Phillips' 1969 book, *The Emerging Republican Majority*, set forth a "Southern strategy" and advised President Nixon that the path forward for Republican success was capitalizing on race. Reagan became an effective spokesperson of the strategy with his attacks on welfare.

In 1975, the conservative writer Irving Kristol, whom many consider the godfather of neo-conservatism, wrote an influential *Wall Street Journal* opinion piece, "The War Against the Cities," that blamed the fiscal problems of cities on progressive notions of integration by invoking explicitly racist arguments. "Why," he asked, "should working-class families, whether white or black, send their children to schools with slum kids who are—as many slum kids, black and white, usually are— rough, tough and delinquent?" He further asked,

❝ *'Small government'*

is simply code for

no more assistance to

poor people, particularly

poor people of color." [23]

— LEE ATWATER,
Reagan Advisor

"And why should working-class and middle-class families move into new apartment houses or projects where one-third of the apartments are reserved by law for welfare families?"

Willie Horton, a prisoner paroled by Massachusetts governor Michael Dukakis, became the symbol of weak-on-crime liberalism that thwarted Dukakis's 1988 presidential campaign (along with an ill-advised video clip of Dukakis in a tank). The infamous Willie Horton TV ad legitimized overt uses of race in political campaigns and helped shift the politics of crime and race to the right for several decades.

How the World Works (continued):
Government is Socialism that Creates a Nation of Dependent "Moochers"

In addition to capturing the word "freedom," conservatives have also captured the term and value of "personal or individual responsibility." They understand that responsibility is a deeply held and widely shared value by individuals, families and communities—from the most conservative to the most progressive. Conservatives, though, have transformed those values into the bedrock of core conservative ideas and values that divides the world between the worthy and self-reliant and the underserving, dependent others.

Conservative economic principles aren't just more effective in their view, they make us better people.

For example, Catholic social philosopher Michael Novak in his 1982 book, *The Spirit of Democratic Capitalism,* claimed that capitalism is, according to *The New York Times,* "a morally superior system based on liberty, individual worth and Judeo-Christian values." [24]

 Capitalism forms morally better people than socialism does. Capitalism teaches people to show initiative and imagination, to work cooperatively in teams, to love and to cherish the law; what is more, it forces persons not only to rely on themselves and their own moral qualities, but also to recognize those moral qualities in others and to cooperate with others freely." [25]

— **Michael Novak**

...

3. Reshape and Realign the American Electorate

The conservative infrastructure that developed ideas and created a drumbeat about government failure and free markets is well known. Less understood is that this infrastructure was always operating at the nexus of policy and politics. Conservative strategists understood that shifting common sense and winning policy campaigns must always be accompanied by a political strategy to weaken and divide opponents and empower and organize supporters.

Organize Discontent:
Strategic Wedge Campaigns that Create Momentum

Ideas succeed in penetrating public consciousness only through action—political campaigns, ballot measures, legislative battles, and media echo chambers that build on latent discontent and bad experiences with government agencies. Everything from potholes to long lines at the DMV are amplified in a constant stream of "government horror stories."

In the wake of Vietnam, Watergate, and 1970s stagflation, generalized discontent with government was ripe for organizing and focusing in a conservative direction. Milton Friedman believed that only a crisis can produce real change. "When that crisis occurs, the actions that are taken depend on the ideas that are lying around," he said.[26]

 *We organize discontent."*

— **HOWARD PHILLIPS**,
*founder of Young Americans for Freedom
and of the Conservative Caucus*[27]

. . .

Parallel and sometimes coordinated efforts drove pockets of discontent from several directions but all toward the antigovernment conventional wisdom described above. For example:

▶ The property-tax revolt was ignited by California Proposition 13 in 1978. Anti-tax campaigns are now an effective component of conservative political action, with deep resonance among broader segments of the electorate.

▶ The 1973 Roe v. Wade decision was the catalyst for social conservatives to create a powerful pro-life political movement fueled by conservative philanthropists and political strategists.

▶ The Gun Control Act of 1968 galvanized a growing number of hardline gun-rights activists; the National Rifle Association (NRA) put new focus on legislative and political action, which led to the first NRA Political Action Committee (PAC), in 1976. The NRA grew rapidly in the ensuring years by effectively threatening that government was coming for your guns.[28]

President Reagan, taking advantage of a backlash against civil rights and Great Society programs, launched a war on welfare and popularized the racist term "welfare queen" to symbolize how government serves the undeserving (black) poor rather than hard-working (white) working- and middle-class Americans.

The attack on government ramped up massively during 1993–94 debate over Bill Clinton's health care reform proposal. Although it included tax subsidies for the insurance industry, to conservatives "Hillarycare" was an attempt to massively expand government involvement in health care. Tens of millions of dollars in advertising and lobbying assailed "government-run health care," and Harry and Louise, the fictional couple that the insurance industry used in effective TV advertisements, won the fight. The fight over the Obamacare individual mandate and tax penalties is a continuation of that same fight.

More recently, public-sector workers,[29] undocumented immigrants, and teachers have been attacked as the "other" who government serves in order to stoke taxpayer resentment, while schools, roads, and other public services deteriorate.

Privatization as a Political Strategy

In 1987, Stuart Butler, a British policy analyst writing for the Heritage Foundation, described how privatization of public services and assets could be used to "reverse the momentum towards ever larger government in the United States." He argued that privatization could alter the fundamental political dynamics that favor increased public (federal) spending:

66 *As long as constituencies see it in their interest to demand government spending, and as long as politicians risk electoral damage when they vote against those demands, it is going to be very difficult to restrain spending. Thus, a strategy to control the size of government needs a powerful "demand-side" element if it is to be successful. Conditions must be created in which the demand for government spending is diverted into the private sector. This is the beauty of privatization. Instead of having to say "no" to constituencies, politicians can adopt a more palatable approach to cutting spending. They can reduce outlays by fostering private alternatives that are more attractive to voters, thereby reducing the clamor for government spending. Changing the political dynamics of government spending in this way is the secret of privatization."[30]*

Political science professor Jeffrey Henig has written extensively about the history of privatization as a political strategy in the latter part of the 20th century.

According to Henig, in addition to "resuscitating laissez faire" economic theory as a precondition for large-scale privatization, the privatization movement masterfully succeeded in reframing existing government contracting practices (common in municipal governments) as a larger theory of practical governance. Thus, standard practice became ideological mission.

During the Reagan years, privatization as an economic theory became privatization as a political strategy to advance a conservative governing agenda of low taxes and smaller government. In the clearest statement of this new approach, the 1988 report of the President's Commission on Privatization[31] concluded with a strong statement in favor of structuring privatization initiatives to create new interest groups with direct stakes in accelerating the process of shrinking the size and scope of government.

> During the Reagan years, privatization as an economic theory became privatization as a political strategy to advance a conservative governing agenda of low taxes and smaller government.

For the Reason Foundation's Robert Poole, it became the perfect incremental strategy. "I figured that if you could gradually build up to socialism, you could probably undo it, dismantling step by step," he said. Government could be dismantled "by privatizing one function after the other, selling each move as justified for its own sake rather than waiting until the majority of the population is convinced of the case for a libertarian utopia".[32]

The Clinton years demonstrated how far the debate about the role of government had shifted. Vice President Al Gore's Commission on Reinventing Government was, on one level, a commitment to bureaucratic reengineering, progressive workforce management, and increasing efficiency of government agencies. But it was also about "cutting government back to basics," privatization, and reducing the size of the workforce at any cost, even though that was often counterproductive. At a deeper level, it was an embrace of market metaphors (public citizens became government's customers), competition as a guiding managerial principle, and an enduring meme about "running government like a business," rather than as a democratic public institution with a commitment to excellence.

Much has been said about the outsourcing of American warfare, but the most profound impact has been to further disconnect Americans with a fundamental role of government—national defense. Dramatically reducing the domestic political and human impact of American wars makes it easier to increase military spending, so that still less is available for public services and programs.

What's the Matter with Kansas?:
Aligning the Right and Building an Energized Base

Republican and donor support of socially conservative movements, with a focus on divisive social issues such as abortion, guns, and gay rights, split key constituencies (e.g., Roman Catholics) from the Democratic Party and aligned social conservatives and evangelicals with economic conservatives.[33] These movements became predictably antigovernment and supportive of free markets. It should be noted, though, that they never supported privatization of Social Security and Medicare, basic universal entitlements.

The Republican Party found common cause with vote rich religious conservatives in their opposition to communism and in their support of what they called "family values" (anti-gay marriage, anti-abortion, etc.)[34] Both abortion rights and gun control proposals were expressions of government attacks on individual freedom.

Alongside the evangelical Right, the National Rifle Association developed into a large and effective grassroots army of antigovernment gun owners to support conservative candidates.

Eliminate the Opposition:
Weaken and Divide Constituencies that Support Public Solutions

The attack on what conservatives in the 1970s believed was the overwhelming political power of liberals became a multi-phased program to politically weaken those progressive forces and politically strengthen conservative constituencies. The conservative ecosphere has been consistently guided by a *political strategy* in advocating their ideas and agenda. Weakening opponents would clear the way to implementing long sought-after policy successes. For example, according to historian Nancy MacLean, "Breaking the spine of the labor movement would hobble any future defense of social security"[35]

These political attacks can be separated into three broad phases:

Phase One was Reagan's rhetorical attacks on government bureaucrats, "welfare queens," his assault on unions and his consistent but unsuccessful attempt to dismantle federally funded legal services for the poor.[36]

Phase Two, beginning on the eve of the George W. Bush presidency, was articulated in 2001 by Grover Norquist as an aggressive strategy to weaken the five "core pillars" of Democratic Party support: unions, trial lawyers, voter registration groups (perpetrating "voter fraud"), big city mayors, and federally funded nonprofits like Planned Parenthood.[37]

> **Individual constituencies and issue-focused groups, seeing no hope of expanding public resources, focused on securing their own portion of a shrinking pie.**

The George W. Bush years further consolidated conservative power by dividing pro-public/pro-government constituencies through a Reaganesque strategy of tax cuts and increased spending on post-911 wars. The Iraq war was the first unfunded war in American history that served to create "useful" budgetary pressures on federal discretionary spending. Individual constituencies and issue-focused groups, seeing no hope of expanding public resources, focused on securing their own portion of a shrinking pie.

Phase Three is Norquist's roadmap in full swing. Conservative attacks in the courts and in state legislatures on public-sector unions and teachers across the country are clear efforts to weaken a political force that advocates for public solutions and public investment. Voting restrictions are bold and transparent—and we now know successful—efforts to suppress the vote of people of color, students and poor people. Defunding Planned Parenthood is a key element of Republican budget and health care legislation.

In an example of the synergy between political and economic power, conservatives have carried out a long-game coordinated attack on defined benefit public sector pensions. Eliminating public sector pensions advances several goals at the same time: reducing government spending, weakening worker commitment to public-sector unions as benefits are reduced, and eliminating worker power to enforce corporate standards through their pension investments.

4. Weaken from Within:
"The government is screwed up; elect me and I'll prove it to you"

Conservative elected officials have had a mission to weaken the institutional
capacity of governments to deliver quality public services and basic health and
safety protections. It's a familiar playbook: hollow out government by cutting
taxes, weakening regulatory enforcement (in part by giving control of regulatory
public functions to industry), and privatizing public services and infrastructure.
And these elected officials have been working to achieve their mission at all levels
of government, from school boards and city councils to state governments and
federal agencies.

The Assault on Regulation

In 1978, economist Murray Weidenbaum published a widely circulated paper
for the American Enterprise Institute (AEI); in it he pointed to federal regulation
as one of the sources of high inflation that was plaguing the economy at the time
and claimed it cost the American economy over $100 billion per year.

In his first year as president, Reagan used that figure and general momentum
towards deregulation to launch a systematic campaign to roll back a long list of
health, safety, consumer, and environmental regulations on business.[38] In 1981,
he charged Vice President George H.W. Bush with creating and leading the
Task Force on Regulatory Relief. Reagan himself kept up a sustained rhetorical
assault on burdensome big government regulations and how they limit freedom.
He appointed industry and anti-regulatory ideologues to lead key agencies. He
reduced funding for regulatory agencies. And, most significantly, he created an
obscure and permanent office, the Office of Information and Regulatory Affairs
(OIRA), within the Office of Management and Budget (OMB), that gave
political control of federal regulatory processes to the White House; by doing
so, he institutionalized cost-benefit analyses as the rubric to evaluate and reject
proposed regulations.

Weakened regulatory enforcement also increases discontent with government.
Ironically, people blame government as well as companies for industry-
caused disasters such as the BP Gulf Oil Spill or the West Texas chemical-
plant explosion. While regulations failed to prevent the disasters, they were
caused entirely by private industry action or inaction. Temporarily they create
demand for increased regulatory oversight, but in the long run they can add to
underlying discontent with government.

Creating the Fiscal Straightjacket:
Deficits and Disinvestment that Weaken Support for Government

In 2001, Grover Norquist talked about "drowning government in a bathtub" but Reagan had already turned a "starve the beast" strategy into a governing reality. Devolution of federal responsibilities to local governments, tax cuts, and increased military spending led to large structural deficits that locked in an American austerity agenda: a vicious cycle of inadequate resources to meet public needs that then drove up discontent about government failure and increased calls for tax cuts. By the end of Reagan's second term, federal assistance to local governments had been cut by 60 percent.[39] As resources dwindled, desperate local and state governments continued to cut budgets and cut costs through contracting out. Austerity and anti-tax politics therefore limited options and action during periods of liberal or progressive governance.

Though cutting taxes had always been a tool of conservative fiscal and economic policy, Reagan made it a centerpiece of his 1980 presidential campaign. But during that period the GOP was also concerned about budget deficits, so when Reagan's earliest tax cuts increased the deficit, Congress and the president reversed course and passed a series of tax increases.

Nonetheless, concerns about budget deficits steadily fell away as the political potency of tax cuts[40] and the political liability of tax increases became evident after George H.W. Bush's reneged on his famous "read my lips — no new taxes" statement. Presidential candidate Bill Clinton used that statement mercilessly in the 1992 presidential campaign. By the time Grover Norquist made his famous bathtub statement, cutting taxes became conservative dogma without regard for the impacts on budget deficits or service levels.

❝ *I don't want to abolish government.*
I simply want to reduce it to the size
where I can drag it into the bathroom
and drown it in the bathtub."

— GROVER NORQUIST,
anti-tax advocate, 2001[41]

5. Take It to the States

 Changing the nation, one state at a time."

— **AMERICANS FOR PROSPERITY FOUNDATION**

...

Conservatives have long understood the importance of controlling state governments.[42] Over the past several decades state legislatures have steadily shifted toward conservative rule, punctuated by national backlash moments in 2006 and 2008, which rolled back conservative gains. But since the beginning of the 21st century, conservative forces have been making significant investments in state-level field organizing. In 2016, the Koch-funded Americans for Prosperity had 650 field staff across the country.

Aided by the Citizens United Supreme Court decision, conservatives are increasingly securing victories in state-level political control and policy. GOP-led legislatures gained control in 2010 of post-census redistricting processes, a crucial step toward locking in GOP majorities of the House of Representatives.

Aided by the Citizens United Supreme Court decision, conservatives are increasingly securing victories in state-level political control and policy.

As of March 2017, Republications controlled thirty-two state legislatures, Democrats controlled fourteen, three were split or tied, and one was unicameral and nonpartisan. Thirty-three governorships were held by Republicans, and twenty-five states were in complete Republican control.

Political Control Over State Legislatures

	DEM	REP	SPLIT+NE
1978	31	11	8
1980	28	15	7
1982	34	10	6
1984	28	10	12
1986	27	9	14
1988	29	8	13
1990	29	6	15
1992	26	7	17
1994	22	15	13
1996	20	17	13
1998	20	17	13
2000	16	18	16
2002	16	21	13
2004	19	20	11
2006	23	16	11
2008	27	14	9
2010	27	14	9
2012	15	27	8
2014	19	26	5
2016	14	32	4

Source: Nick Hillman, University of Wisconsin-Madison[43]

State control has also provided a beachhead against the new progressive federalism, as urban community-labor movements passed local policies on minimum wages, paid leave, menu labeling, plastic-bag bans, firearm regulations, and more. State after state under GOP control has passed preemption laws, eliminating the legal authority of local governments to act on these issues.

Conclusion

The strategic elements described above have clearly added up to significant changes in American politics, society, culture and the economy. It wasn't a straight line, nor a command and control directed campaign, but it does show that there were significant forces who were playing the long game— thinking strategically, operating at the nexus of ideas, policy and politics and with clarity about the nation they want to create.

The basic trajectory is clear. They achieved a steady erosion of support for government action and public solutions and an equally steady concentration of wealth, power and influence over the things that matter to us all.

They played the long game. Part 2 that follows is a discussion of what a long game for progressives could look like.

...

❝ *The path to a society that values common goods and the common welfare, that reimagines politics as an arena of deliberation rather than an advertising-fueled field of consumer choice, needs all the political work and imagination progressives can muster."*

— **DANIEL RODGERS**, *Princeton University*

...

PART 2 LOOKING AHEAD: FINDING THE LONG GAME

66 *'Public' stood not just for how something was financed — with the tax dollars of citizens — but for a communal ownership of institutions and for a society that privileged the common good over individual advancement."*

— **NIKOLE HANNAH-JONES**,
The New York Times [44]

So how do we build a movement for the common good? Progressive campaigns have won impressive victories, but progressives lack clarity and unity of purpose as well as a shared coherent governing philosophy. And the progressive infrastructure doesn't have a consistent practice of thinking about ideas and the long-game strategy. It's a real problem and fundamentally limits our potential to reshape American democracy.

The following ideas are intended to stimulate discussion and debate and to lead to *a practice of the long game*. Such a practice is not about figuring out *the* long-term strategy or *the* policy agenda, nor about planning specific campaigns, tending to organizational interests, or fundraising. Rather, it's about creating spaces, trust, and free discussion of ideas and strategies. It will require the discomfort of thinking bigger and longer term than we normally do (alone or together), honest assessments of what it will take to succeed, and a hard look at our own failures and weaknesses. A practice of the long game ensures responsiveness to new developments, new ideas, and the dynamic nature of time.

It's worth repeating: Public distrust of and even disdain for government action (and the flip side of the coin, the belief in so-called free markets) are now defining features of American politics, manifest in every election, every policy campaign and every public debate on the issues of the day.

Understanding the strategy the Right has pursued to redefine the role of government is a critical part of developing a response, as is a clear and forceful restatement of the comprehensive case for effective government. But those are only the first steps. Now we need a way forward.

Where We Are: An Honest Assessment

Many winning campaigns and bold actions across the country are challenging the power of the financial industry, raising wages and living standards for workers, raising funds for public investments, combating racism, and more. These kinds of actions and successes move the ball forward.

But without knowing where we're heading and what kind of country we want to create, and without a conscious strategy, fundamental progress will be accidental at

We are winning battles but still losing the war.

best. Despite many inspiring campaign successes, in the last several decades distrust of government has only increased, as has conservative control of state governments across the country. We are winning battles but still losing the war.

The focus on issues and campaigns is the double-edged sword that, on one hand, directs action and organizing toward concrete accomplishment but, on the other, obscures the need for coherent long-term ideas and strategies. We simply have to do both.

The progressive infrastructure too often seems to be a collection of issues and campaigns (policy and electoral) competing for foundation and labor-movement dollars. That competition, while perhaps ultimately unsolvable, has real consequence for movement coherence and works against the kind of long term strategy and alignment needed to shift public attitudes and reshape American democracy.

The plethora of organizations, the competition for funding and the siloed campaign focus of the progressive infrastructure masks a much more significant challenge for the progressive movement. There are few large civic institutions that keep large numbers of progressive people connected in ways that establish common bonds, experiences, and values. The Right has used Rotary clubs, chambers of commerce, churches, and issue groups with enthusiastic membership (e.g., the NRA and the pro-life organizations) to reach and organize millions of people. Progressives don't have the same kind of broad civic infrastructure to reach large numbers of people on a regular basis. Unions may be the only remaining large-membership institutions within the progressive ecosystem; unfortunately, they are declining rapidly in the face of conservative efforts.

We also need to acknowledge that progressives represent a complicated mix of beliefs, attitudes, experiences, and interests. There are differences and divisions between progressives who focus on social issues and racial issues and those who focus on economic issues. But it should be crystal clear today that issues of race, gender and class are intertwined and completely inseparable. Any other interpretation will consign progressives to become a series of cul-de-sacs in American culture and politics, incapable of becoming a governing majority.

Ian Haney-Lopez and Robert Reich argue that the way forward requires that progressives *"develop a narrative about how political opportunists have used race and gender to divide us, to demonize government in the eyes of many working-class whites, and to prevent us from joining together in a broad-based coalition to fight widening inequalities of income, wealth, and political power. [Progressives] must re-tell the story of the last 50 years, emphasizing how race and other culture-war issues have been used to divide and conquer."* [45]

It should be crystal clear today that issues of race, gender and class are intertwined and completely inseparable.

We've seen the success of recent movements (i.e. Fight for Fifteen, Black Lives Matter, Occupy,) to lift critical issues into mainstream public discourse. These campaigns and efforts put a spotlight on the issues of race and class, but to initiate real change they must also be informed by and able to articulate a progressive governing philosophy and a coherent pro-democracy reform agenda, one that offers public solutions from responsive, inclusive, and effective government institutions.

The Importance and Urgency of Silo-Busting

The conservative agenda and strategy described above is, at its core, an assault on government in order to assert private power over public goods. Racism, attacks on unions and many other conservative initiatives have been important means to an end: restructuring American democracy, governance and the economy in reinforcing mechanisms that institutionalize that control as depicted in the chart that follows.

Conservative Mechanisms Restructuring American Democracy

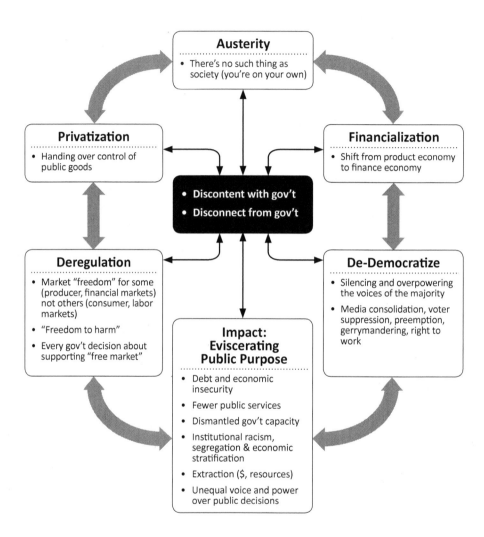

There is a great deal discussion among progressive funders and leaders about
the constraints of issue and organizational silos. "Silo-busting" starts with an
understanding of who and what we are competing with so that leaders and activists
understand the synergy and interconnectedness between these mechanisms rather
than as distinct issue silos. This is *not* to argue that every campaign take on all of
these issues—but to ensure that we are adding it up to a new governing vision and
an enduring movement willing and able to lead and govern.

All is Not Lost, but We've Got a Long Way to Go

Progressives have struggled with a fundamental political paradox: on the one hand, there's widespread public support for specific public programs and actions that provide benefits for people, while on the other hand there's little support for government in general as an institution for solving our problems. In other words, Americans are "programmatically" liberal yet "ideologically" conservative.

For example, by wide margins Americans support universal health care, the minimum wage, strong regulations on financial industry, background checks for gun owners and are worried about climate change and the influence of money in politics.[46] But, trust in government— the only institution that can solve those problems—is at all-time lows.

Trust in government — the only institution that can solve those problems — is at all-time lows.

The good news is that the public expresses far greater confidence in their local governments than in the executive and legislative branches in Washington. A 2016 Gallup poll[47] found that 71 percent of Americans trust local governments to handle problems, and 62 percent trust state governments. (Only 13 percent of Americans approve of Congress, the lowest confidence in any institution Gallup tests.)

How much trust and confidence to you have in...
% Great deal/Fair amount of trust

■ *The local governments in the area where you live when it comes to handling local problems?*
■ *The government of the state where you live when it comes to handling state problems?*

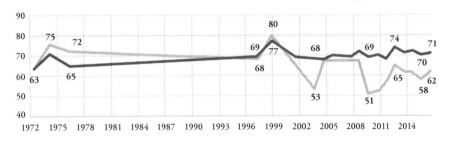

Gallup

It's also instructive to compare attitudes towards the federal government among urban, suburban and rural populations. According to a 2015 *Washington Post* analysis[48] of Pew data[49], "People who live in urban areas (28 percent) are slightly more likely to trust the federal government than those who live in rural areas

(22 percent)." Interestingly, the urban/rural split disappears regarding faith in local government: 41 percent of urban residents and 40 percent of rural residents trust their local government to solve problems. (Note: inconsistency between 2015 and 2016 attitudes towards local government are due to different questions used. We include to show urban/rural comparison.)

It is, of course, too early to gauge the long-term impact of the Trump presidency and GOP control of the House and Senate, but it's safe to assume that Americans are increasingly looking away from Washington to solve their problems.

There's further evidence of greater trust in local governments and support for identifiable public programs in the actions of local voters. In the November 2016 election, voters across the country passed tax measures to fund important services and several hundred billion dollars in bond measures to invest in local infrastructure in both red and blue states. For example:

- ▶ Thirty-four transit bonds passed (two-thirds of all those on the ballot), raising billions of dollars for important public transit infrastructure projects.[50]

- ▶ Voters adopted large numbers of bond measures for affordable housing, water infrastructure, and school construction and renovation. Wisconsin alone passed fifty-three local school bond measures.[51]

- ▶ A number of municipalities passed sales, income, and soda taxes to pay for preschools, K–12 schools, health programs, homeless services, community colleges, and even general city revenues to fund basic services.

Additionally, the growth of "the Resistance" in the wake of the Trump election has been inspiring and impressive; it has the potential to become the core of a new pro-public movement—but only *if* we seize the opportunity for the long run.

Ten Strategies for Progress

The following are ten possible strategies to mount an effective long-game response. Each is intended as a point of departure for further discussion.

1. Reclaim Freedom: Reengage in the Battle of Ideas

❝ *Ideas shape people's understanding of the world, which in turn shapes beliefs about what is possible, economic aspirations and political expectations.*"

—**THOMAS PALLEY**, *Economist*[52]

. . .

For a movement to lead and govern American public institutions, it must have a clear notion of the fundamental role of government and how it would define and deliver on the common good for the majority. Unfortunately, progressives are neither clear nor unified in the appropriate role they see for government, for markets, and what it means to be a responsible citizen in a democratic society.

We need more than a laundry list of issues and policies. We need a governing philosophy that describes how the world works and the role that government institutions and action should play. Competing worldviews boil down to the different conceptions of freedom and responsibility described in the first part of this paper. We need to assert a progressive view of freedom, our vision of how government institutions must advance and protect those ideals and show how imbalances of power are in the way of the pursuit of freedom.

We also must redefine and reclaim responsibility as a core progressive value— individual, community and corporate responsibility. At its core that means we all (individuals, public officials, corporate and business leaders) take responsibility for the impacts of our actions, clean up after ourselves and we do our part to create a healthy functioning society. It shouldn't be difficult. Every day we learn of cases where corporations create "externalities" such as air and water pollution, unsafe workplaces and even poverty that the rest of us have to address because they are failing in these basic responsibilities. When they talk about burdensome government regulations we should simply insist that responsible Americans clean up after themselves.

We need to assert a progressive view of freedom, our vision of how government institutions must advance and protect those ideals and show how imbalances of power are in the way of the pursuit of freedom.

While there is some generalized disdain for free-market capitalism among progressive activists, there isn't a clearly articulated alternative. We need an ideology and an economic theory to convincingly demonstrate that democratic public institutions and public power (e.g. regulatory, social insurance) are uniquely capable of doing what needs to be done to advance and protect the common good and that markets alone are inherently incapable of delivering basic public goods. A few examples:

- ▶ FedEx can deliver packages, but it won't deliver an envelope to any address in the United States for the same price.

- ▶ Auto companies can build cars, but they need rules to ensure our air isn't polluted.

- ▶ Health insurers sell policies to those who can afford them, but only government can ensure that every American has access to health care.

Beyond a governing philosophy, we should be able to describe the role and purpose of government in American democracy. For example, here's one view of those basic roles:

- ▶ Provide public services that we all rely upon to live, work, play, and become educated, productive members of society

- ▶ Provide subsidies and investments that grow the economy and give everyone a fair shot at a decent life

- ▶ Regulate corporate and individual behavior to prevent excessive concentrations of power and exploitation, to create shared prosperity, and to protect public health, safety, and the planet

- ▶ Promote public safety and fair justice

- ▶ Protect and ensure equal human and civil rights

We can, and should, reeducate Americans about good things government has done while playing each of these roles (some better than others) but, especially given popular distrust of governments, we first must reclaim the very idea of the "public"— that there are important things we can and must do together. Conservatives exalt the *idea* of the "free market" first and the virtues of business second. We need to do the same: first articulate and exalt public purpose and then advocate for effective action by government institutions.

This is not about creating one manifesto or one hot new idea. It must be about reinvigorating a healthy practice of debate and dialogue about ideas as a central aspect of movement building, rather than as a peripheral activity of a few thinkers. It must be a commitment by the entire progressive infrastructure to engage each other, learn together, and create spaces and times to discuss and debate ideas and governing philosophies and how they connect with current conditions, policy campaigns, and action.

> **We can, and should, reeducate Americans about good things government has done but, we first must reclaim the very idea of the "public"— that there are important things we can and must do together.**

That is the only way to come up with a widely shared set of aims and ideals among a diverse and geographically dispersed progressive ecosystem of strategists, leaders, organizers, activists and organizations across the country. Unfortunately, most progressive conferences, convenings, and discussions focus on specific issues, campaigns, and organizing structures. These events depend on assumptions about common ideas, but real ideological differences may be at play.

We can change that by acting as if ideas matter in the long run as much as the campaigns we take on by first being clear about the larger ideas those campaigns advance.

2. Keep Up the Assault on Failed Ideas *(and the interests that they serve)*

For decades, the Right has remained focused on three key tasks: delegitimize government (ideologically and practically), exalt markets and business as "job creators," and take control of the institutions of government. Progressives also need multiple tracks. We must lift up the need for public action (to regulate, invest, and protect) but also vigorously discredit the failed economic theories and rhetoric while exposing the self-interest that led to, funded and benefited from the attack on government that has dominated politics for the last forty-plus years.

Corporate and ideological interests have long argued that reducing taxes on the wealthy will "trickle down" to create shared economic growth and that virtually any substantial, progressive change in public policy will kill jobs, create a stifling government bureaucracy, or curtail economic growth. Every public policy that we now take for granted was bitterly fought by economic interests trying to protect their revenues, profits and market shares using these same arguments: food and safety regulations adopted in 1906 and updated in later years, the minimum wage established in 1938 (and every subsequent increase), progressive taxes, consumer product safety, Medicare and Social Security and every other consumer, financial, workplace and environmental piece of legislation.

There is plenty of evidence that conservatives and business groups have been "crying wolf." There are plenty of real-world examples showing conclusively that minimum-wage increases didn't kill jobs, tax increases didn't cause businesses to flee or stunt massive economic growth, and the regulation of toxic pollutants didn't destroy industries. And the evidence keeps coming. Just look at the so-called Kansas "miracle," where massive tax cuts and privatization that conservative and business leaders claimed would stimulate economic growth failed to do so and produced deep cuts in K–12 education and other popular public services.[53]

One report won't bust myths or offer the ultimate proof, nor can a single organizational program broadcast those reports widely and consistently enough to make a difference; rather, we need an all-hands-on-deck effort, one that's integrated into everything we do. We need a consistent drumbeat of real-world examples of right-wing ideological failures. But we should go beyond simply refuting and citing facts and include ridiculing a century of false claims in popular culture, so their "crying wolf" claims are dismissed out of hand.

3. Turn *Our* Ideas and Values into a New Conventional Wisdom

John Kenneth Galbraith has written extensively about how crucial worldview and conventional wisdom are to shifting economic power. The following two quotations sum up his perspective:

66 *The emancipation of belief is the most formidable task of reform and the one on which all else depends."*

"The power of the [corporation] depends on instilling the belief that any public or private action that serves its purposes also serves the purposes of the public at large." [54]

Conventional wisdom is the popular expression of values, beliefs and ideas that define the nation's politics and culture. It embodies common understanding of how the world works (influential conservative writer Jude Wanniski even wrote a book called *How the World Works*), and it dictates who the winners and losers are in society and in the economy. It is both created and confirmed by the ideas we advance, and it drives how we interpret current events.

Just as Ayn Rand's fictional accounts portray an extreme libertarian ideal of freedom in ways millions could relate to, progressives need to articulate a pro-public vision that resonates with how people believe the world works. Rand's vision is based upon a deep and somewhat dark view of human nature that portrays how people relate to the world and society around them—who we trust, who we don't, who we believe has virtue and who doesn't. These core beliefs create the foundation the define popular attitudes and ideology about government and upon which people make political choices. We have different beliefs and we should talk about them.

Progressives also need to ensure that individual campaigns and projects collectively create a new widely shared common sense about the failure of conservative ideas, the ideas that advance the common good, and the obstacles to a country that benefits us all. Public-opinion research can provide useful insights about public beliefs, values and attitudes on many subjects, but we should start by getting clear about our own beliefs and the conventional wisdom we'd like to "create" over the long run. These are some of my own basic beliefs about the way the world works— and there probably others we could include:

- ▶ The extreme concentration of wealth weakens our democracy, hurts Americans and divides us as a nation.

- ▶ Only government can ensure that public goods—health care, economic security, education, communications, transportation, open space, and more—are available to every American.

- ▶ We are citizens, not simply consumers of individual public services. We have obligations, responsibilities, and rights.

- ▶ As citizens we must pay for the things we value as a society and not only for the specific services we receive.

- ▶ Markets can't deliver goods and services unless people have funds to purchase them, therefore, markets alone can't provide important public goods (i.e. health care) that should be available to everyone.

▶ Economies grow when people have money to spend.

▶ Corporations and businesses can earn a profit, but not if it harms the country.

▶ Markets and the economy need rules — on their own they cause problems that impact us all.

▶ Diversity and inclusion makes us stronger as a nation, more economically prosperous, and better as people.

▶ We do well individually and collectively when everyone does well.

The goal shouldn't necessarily to find <u>the</u> list and even these could perhaps be stated more clearly, but what is important is for us to understand that our ideas, actions and campaigns need to add up to a new set of widely shared beliefs about how the world works.

In the fall of 2011, gearing up for a tough campaign for U.S Senate, Elizabeth Warren articulated a worldview that inspired millions:

66 *There is nobody in this country who got rich on their own. Nobody. You built a factory out there — good for you. But I want to be clear. You moved your goods to market on roads the rest of us paid for. You hired workers the rest of us paid to educate. You were safe in your factory because of police forces and fire forces that the rest of us paid for. You didn't have to worry that marauding bands would come and seize everything at your factory... Now look. You built a factory and it turned into something terrific or a great idea — God bless! Keep a hunk of it. But part of the underlying social contract is you take a hunk of that and pay forward for the next kid who comes along."*

In his 2012 presidential campaign, Barack Obama gave his version of what government is for:

66 *If you were successful, somebody along the line gave you some help. There was a great teacher somewhere in your life. Somebody helped to create this unbelievable American system that we have that allowed you to thrive. Somebody invested in roads and bridges. If you've got a business—you didn't build that. Somebody else made that happen. The Internet didn't get invented on its own. Government research created the Internet so that all the companies could make money off the Internet."*

The point is, is that when we succeed, we succeed because of our individual initiative, but also because we do things together. There are some things, just like fighting fires, we don't do on our own. I mean, imagine if everybody had their own fire service. That would be a hard way to organize fighting fires.

So we say to ourselves, ever since the founding of this country, you know what, there are some things we do better together. That's how we funded the GI Bill. That's how we created the middle class. That's how we built the Golden Gate Bridge or the Hoover Dam. That's how we invented the Internet. That's how we sent a man to the moon. We rise or fall together as one nation and as one people, and that's the reason I'm running for President — because I still believe in that idea. You're not on your own, we're in this together." [55]

4. Be Defenders and Reformers, not Attackers

Many people assume that all we really need to do is educate people about the government services and protections we take for granted every day. It's a long list.[56] The paint in our homes used to have lead, cars were unsafe, and pesticides poisoned us before new laws were passed. The GPS on our phones wasn't created by Apple or Google— the government invented it, owns the satellites, and makes it freely accessible.

But this approach has potential pitfalls. For example, when we remind people that the roads are publicly funded, they don't necessarily think about how they love the roads. They are more likely to think about potholes and traffic. They might even think the private sector could do it better. And many view government only through its failures such as police shootings of black men, inadequate public schools, lead poisoning in our water systems and corrupt public officials.

. . .

 Believers in liberal democracy have unilaterally disarmed in the defense of the institution." [58]

— **STEVEN PINKER**, *Professor of Psychology at Harvard*

. . .

We have to talk (a lot) about the many things government action has done effectively. If we don't, the idea of public solutions and government action has no defenders. You can't win a battle when there's only one side, especially with the constant stream of public failures, corruption scandals, and general ugliness of political campaigns.

On the other hand, we can't be the defenders of a status quo that most people don't like and that falls short in significant ways. The right wing has repeatedly attacked the idea and institutions of government, while the progressive movement has left the idea and successes of government action undefended. It's possible—and essential—to be both pro-public and pro-reform.

We also must acknowledge the implicit cooperation of progressives in solidifying distrust of government after LBJ's lies about Vietnam, Nixon's abuse of power, and the actions of industry-connected and antigovernment public officials since then.

We must figure out how to talk about government failures and corruption without reinforcing negative attitudes toward the idea of government.

Even some progressive advocacy campaigns today increase this distrust by focusing on the real failures of government institutions and representatives— police violence and abuse against people of color, mass incarceration, regulatory capture, wars, and corruption. For example, while it's critically important to wage campaigns that expose and challenge corporate and Wall Street control of public institutions, doing so fosters cynicism and the (well-deserved) belief that governments serve the powerful—another source of discontent.

We clearly are up against strong headwinds if our goal is to rebuild trust in public institutions. There are, and will always be, many examples of government failures – whether by incompetence, corruption, poor judgment, regulatory capture by industry, or ideologically driven policy decisions. There is no easy answer, but we should recognize that cases of corruption by politicians from any political party and government failures of all types further the popular beliefs that all politicians are corrupt and all government workers are incompetent.

We have two basic challenges.

First, we must figure out how to talk about government failures and corruption without reinforcing negative attitudes toward the idea of government and public solutions. We must approach our work with clarity—to make crucial distinctions between the real failures of government agencies (with limits that are human, political, financial, and bureaucratic), corporate control of government institutions, and the larger idea of public solutions. Without making these distinctions, we lose sight of our real goal: to win control of public institutions with a broad mandate to transform government institutions and create policies and programs that advance the common good.

Second, we need to become the reformers if we want to have credibility with the American people. We need an agenda that creates effective, responsive, inclusive, and innovative government institutions. And we also must be about accountability, efficiency, openness, cutting waste, and stopping corruption. Ultimately, though, it's not about credibility but about whether governments deliver quality services, economic prosperity, and health and safety for the American people.

The Trump administration will only further weaken the effectiveness of and support for public institutions, filling government agency positions with ideologues, industry representatives, and inexperienced people from the conservative base. This will only create more urgency to advocate a pro-public set of values and reforms without further damaging support for the idea and institution of government.

5. Distinguish Between the Control of Government and the Democratic Idea of Government

Too often we talk about government failure in a way that subtly reinforces the separation between us (the people) and the government institutions that act on our behalf. Though we know that the idea of government is not equivalent to who is in control at any given time, we don't always keep the separation squarely in mind. Our lack of clarity complicates the task of competing to control and create governments that work for all of us, not just the wealthy and powerful.

What happens in government is about the exercise of power — there's always a *who*.

When we talk about "the government" or refer to things the "government did" we divert our attention from the people and forces in control of government.[57] We obscure the fact that the decisions and actions of those in government serve powerful interests who receive tangible benefits from that control. What happens in government is about the exercise of power — there's always a *who*.

Failure to make these distinctions and offer a clear set of public values and a reform agenda can add to the discontent towards government and the generalized sense that government always serves someone else—as fact—as opposed to a result of concerted political action.

We are up against powerful and wealthy forces that seek to control government institutions and action in order to increase their power and wealth. We must continue to expose those interests and the impacts of their power over public goods on individuals, communities and the nation. But that's not enough. We also have to do far more to show the power and successes that public control over public goods has delivered over time and the public institutions that are essential to exercising that control.

Too often advocates, organizations and the press fail to point to those successes either because they were incomplete successes (as they always are,) or because they happened decades ago and are now simply taken for granted. When we do talk about positive legislative or regulatory action from the past it's almost always when it comes under attack from conservative or industry forces. That's too late.

6. Add It Up to More than the Sum of Its Parts

As mentioned above, campaigns are winning important things — raising wages, investing in communities, reducing greenhouse emissions, expanding opportunities for people coming out of prison and much more. But in themselves, these victories don't break through issue silos, educate about larger ideas about public purpose nor add up to a new conventional wisdom. Without a conscious effort, we remain swamped by the ideology of the market and distrust of government.

Simply stated, individual issues and campaigns must add up to more than the sum of their parts.

We should start with the facts. Government action to level the playing field and balance the pursuit of private profit and power with the common good is the *essential element* in every progressive initiative. For example: living wage campaigns use the power of government purchasing to lift economic standards; inclusionary housing policies employ the land use power of government to increase the amount of affordable housing; mass-transit systems rely on public spending of tax dollars; Social Security and Medicare depend on the government's unique ability to create universal social-insurance programs; the

Clean Air Act and the Pure Food and Drug Act that protect public health rely on the regulatory powers of the state. These are the essential public powers that have created every policy victory from National Labor Relations Act to banking reform, and much more.

And it's important to acknowledge that every one of these advances happened because of concerted action by millions of ordinary people. It's what we do.

But broadly shared clarity about these facts is only the first step. We have to operate differently. We are never going to be able to match, dollar for dollar, the interests who want to weaken government. And we must recognize that we are in difficult air space: negative political campaigns that alienate, scandals

> **Government action is the *essential element* in every progressive initiative.**

involving elected officials of both parties, and the inevitable and understandable reaction to the results of austerity, deregulation, privatization, financialization and institutionalized racism.

So, what does adding it up look like?

- ▶ When faced with national legislative battles such as preventing the repeal of Obamacare, expanding Medicare coverage to include larger segments of the public or responding to national crises like the hurricanes in Puerto Rico and Houston, adding it up means organizations, leaders, and millions of activists can weigh in with a unified agenda at the right moments and in the right places across the country—in red, purple, and blue states.

- ▶ Over the long term, individual issues and campaigns add up to a set of ideas and new conventional wisdom about governments and markets (as described in steps numbers one and two, above).

- ▶ Progressive governing principles are embedded deeply in the rules and functioning of government action at all levels.

If we could redesign the organizational structure of the progressive movement from the ground up, based on what we know now, it would doubtless look different. But we can't do that. We have to work within infrastructure we have: Therefore, confronting the power imbalance we face can only happen with an unprecedented level of alignment, cooperation, and coordination among progressives around a coherent set of ideas about the role of government, the economy, and political strategy.

This doesn't require that every progressive join every campaign and coalition. But it does require that we all are walking and talking in the same direction, with a clear sense of where we're going and how we might get there. If we are to compete for governing power and a new conventional wisdom, then we need far more strategic, organizational, and ideological coherence that can begin to add it up. Otherwise it just won't happen. And as mentioned in the introduction to this section, it's an ongoing process not a static manifesto. Times change, we learn by doing, and most things are not under our control.

We should start with a far greater commitment to educating leaders, organizers and activists about the ideas, history and facts mentioned above—not just once but as a standard part of everything we do.

And we should create spaces where progressive leaders, organizers, and funders can grapple seriously with the organizational challenges and dynamics that prevent more synergy, more expansive collaboration, and ultimately greater short, medium and especially long-term impact.

7. Embrace Strategic Incrementalism: Chart a Path Toward the Future We Want

Milton Friedman understood—and embraced—strategic incrementalism. He saw that policy solutions were steps in extended processes of transition, from what is to what should be: "You cannot simply describe the utopian solution, and leave it to somebody else how we get from here to there... It is irresponsible, immoral I would say, simply to say, 'Oh well, somehow or other we'll overnight drop the whole thing.' You have to have some mechanism of going from here to there." [59]

❝ *It is of course desirable to have a vision of the idea, of Utopia. Far be it from me to denigrate that. But we can't stop there. If we do, we become a cult or a religion, and not a living, vital force."*

— MILTON FRIEDMAN [60]

...

Friedman is credited with developing the idea of school vouchers, an idea we have seen unfolding over the past several decades. For him vouchers were the Trojan Horse that would eventually eliminate government-run schools entirely. While the approach shifted toward charter schools in the wake of high-profile political failures of voucher initiatives, eventually vouchers made their comeback. But that is still only a step towards his long-term vision. As he explained, "I have long supported and pushed the voucher plan for schooling as well as the negative income tax in welfare. In both cases I do so not because these are necessarily part of my utopian society but because they seem to me the most effective steps, given where we are, in moving toward where we want to go."[61]

What do we mean by "strategic incrementalism?"

▶ As Milton Friedman said it starts with knowing where we're going in the long run.

▶ It's carrying out campaigns that create momentum and conditions that lay the foundation for the next step in several ways. A policy victory can realign economic and market forces, restructure the rules and structures of how public agencies work and establish policies and programs that have broad based political support.

▶ It's carrying out successful campaigns that realign constituencies and where larger numbers of people across party, regional and demographic lines will fight to protect and expand.

Sometimes progressive campaigns are focused entirely on concrete victories—small and large—without a clear path towards the larger transformation that we seek. Those are good and important advances but in themselves don't restructure markets, change policy and regulatory regimes nor realign political constituencies.

Other times we focus on an aspirational policy goal but don't have a strategy for ultimate success. Single-payer healthcare is an example. One of the most important of public functions, it would be a radical transformation of one sixth of the economy and would take on some of the most powerful forces in society. Medicare was the first step; the public option could have been the second step.

Obamacare, although a complicated program that accommodated powerful insurance and pharmaceutical industries, was absolutely a step forward towards universal health insurance. GOP efforts to repeal it were thwarted precisely because large numbers of working and middle-class people in both red and blue regions gained health insurance through Medicaid expansion, uninsured young adults can now stay on their parents' plan and people with pre-existing conditions can now access affordable care without restrictions and exorbitant premiums. The bottom line is that millions more have health insurance today.

DACA is also a case in point. Comprehensive immigration reform hasn't happened, though DACA, because it impacted large numbers of people from different class backgrounds, has created pressure to reinstate the program in the wake of the recent administration action.

And still other times we fail to address critical structural and policy obstacles that have broad impacts across many issue areas so don't fall into one silo. For example, private companies of all kinds argue against disclosing vital public information claiming that it would expose "trade secrets" to their competitors. The Freedom of Information Act includes an exemption for companies to protect trade secrets, but companies go much further and refuse to disclose basic information that impacts important public services, and health, safety, consumer and environmental protections. Also, cost-benefit analyses (often flawed) that are now basic requirements of all new regulatory acts often create overwhelming obstacles to creating life and planet saving safeguards.

Of course, there's no magic formula that can point to *the one* correct path. There's always a choice in individual campaigns—how far to go, when to recognize and accept progress and when to hold out for more. The consequences of those choices are real and can last for decades. For example, President Richard Nixon proposed a near-universal health care system based upon an employer mandate and subsidies for those who couldn't afford insurance. A young Senator Ted Kennedy, who advocated a single-payer system, was willing to accept Nixon's proposal but couldn't get the support of significant constituencies, who thought they could do better. They couldn't, and they didn't.[62]

Obviously, incremental progress can be rolled back and certainly don't guarantee further progress.

We won't always have a clear path forward. That shouldn't be a reason not to act but there are a few things that can be done to improve our chances of long-term success:

1. Campaigns should start by plotting out and visualizing a strategic path (or paths) to larger success beyond the specific campaign objective.

2. Organizations should identify key structural and regulatory barriers to their success in the short, medium and long term and develop ideas and strategies

to address them. These barriers almost always impact a range of reform and policy areas so cross organizational and constituency partnerships are essential.

8. Build the Base: Gain Power through Numbers

Progressives often talk about "building power." This broad, poorly defined term masks the essential determining characteristic of power — whether you have it or not.

Conservatives are clear about their central task: to govern. But it wasn't always that way. In 1980, conservative direct-mail expert and New Right leader Richard Viguerie said, "New Right conservatives believe that we will govern America. A lot of older conservatives did not see themselves as winning and governing America. They saw themselves as sometimes influencing those who governed, but they did not see themselves as governing."[63]

They certainly get it now. They focused on *competing for power*, particularly at the state and federal level, and now they have it in many places.

Nonetheless, major hurdles remain:

▶ Progressive organizing groups don't come near the scale of total union membership. Several national networks are initiating door-to-door canvasses and membership recruitment, a good start.

▶ Existing organization, while changing, is still far too concentrated on the coasts. There are promising signs with new efforts in a growing number of urban areas in red and purple states; these hubs should also serve as anchors of regional, multi-racial organizing that can reach large numbers of people in cities, suburbs, and smaller towns.

▶ We've seen recently that large numbers of people are willing to take action, but competing for power requires millions of people in relationship through organizations that keep them connected for ongoing political and economic education and periodic action. Progressives simply lack the kind of deep, lay-level connections to the same kinds of institutions like evangelical churches and movements that conservatives have.

▶ Hundreds (maybe thousands) of progressive organizations across the country focus on a variety of issues and campaigns and employ different organizational models. The very real competition for funding among these organizations presents obstacles to cooperation and distracts from the task of building large membership bases.

We may or may not be able to gather the resources to staff up to the scale and breadth of organizing needed. Either way, we have to challenge ourselves about whether existing resources are deployed in the most effective way possible—between national and local organizations and between the myriad single-issue and multi-issue organizations working in regions and states across the country.

We've seen some promising signs that our reach is capable of growing. For example, in the wake of the 2016 presidential election, the breadth, scale, and energy of the Women's March took the progressive infrastructure—and the nation—by surprise. The organic growth of thousands of volunteer-led Indivisible[64] and Black Lives Matters chapters shows a hunger for organizing, connecting, and taking action. Mass grassroots action repeatedly thwarted GOP efforts to repeal Obamacare. And broad-based reaction against racism, while driven by tragedy, has stimulated a long-needed national discussion about race and sparked grassroots action across the country.

The Fall 2017 election results certainly show hopeful signs and point to the potential for a growing urban and suburban alignment on issues and politics. But those same elections also point to a hardening of conservative voting patterns in rural and small town America that create real obstacles to state legislative success.[65]

We need to start with an honest, rigorous, and sober picture of an institutional base big enough, broad enough, strong enough and capable enough to compete to lead and govern America. We don't have that picture now and we certainly don't have that reach, geographically, demographically, or institutionally. Labor unions have the largest self-funded and self-identified memberships but no longer have the scale and breadth needed to fully drive a progressive renewal and compete for governing power. And after the expected Supreme Court ruling in Janus v. AFSCME Council 31, resources and membership will decline even further.

The bottom line is that making real progress requires being in power. And winning power requires talking to lots and lots of people—not just through social media, but actually talking. In addition to needing a long game and a sophisticated and aligned progressive infrastructure, we desperately need more real organizing and powerful institutions (unions and others) with large, active, and self-identified memberships and effective leaders in cities and states across the country.

9. Culture and Music Aren't the Add-ons — They Are the Heart and Soul.

 Songs change hearts, hearts change minds, minds change people and

people change the world." [66]

—**MARY GAUTHIER**, *Folk Singer*

. . .

There is no doubt that culture — music, film, television, theater, literature, photography, and visual art — plays a central role in shaping public attitudes and beliefs about human nature, how the world works and who are the "good guys" and who are the "bad guys" in society.

Conservatives have long understood the power of popular culture. In 1947, Ayn Rand was hired by Hollywood business and entertainment leaders to write a guide book to root out ideas and language that radical, "collectivist" Hollywood screenwriters were inserting into film scripts.

 Politics is not a separate field in itself. Political ideas do not come out

*of thin air. They are the result of the **moral premises** which men have*

accepted. Whatever people believe to be the good, right and proper

human actions — that will determine their political opinions."

— **AYN RAND**,
*Screen Guide for Americans, for The Motion Picture Alliance for
the Preservation of American Ideals, 1947* [67]

. . .

Culture's impact operates at many levels. There are examples in all these cultural forms throughout American history that have helped create cultural and social norms, have educated and inspired popular movements and have put a spotlight on obscure issues and hidden injustices.

► Jacob Riis' and Lewis Hines' photos of urban poverty in the early 1900s helped create widespread concern and motivation for leaders to act.

► Important documentaries such as *Titicut Follies, An Inconvenient Truth, I'm Not Your Negro* and *Harlan County, USA,* have done the same for a wide range of critical issues.

► Powerful songs such as *We Shall Overcome* fueled civil rights movement action against powerful and violent forces and continue to inspire movements today. Even popular and rock music including older songs like Aretha Franklin's "Respect" and Bob Dylan's "Blowing in the Wind" or modern songs like Beyonce's "Lemonade" have widespread influence in popular culture today.

► Films like *Silkwood, Erin Brockovich, Norma Rae* and *Selma* have educated millions about critical issues and inspire people to action by showing how others have taken courageous actions and led movements to fix injustices.

► And great literature (as far back as the Bible, Greek philosophers and Shakespeare) has left a legacy of universally recognizable stories such as *A Tale of Two Cities* and Orwell's *1984* that create new phrases (i.e. "big brother") that we refer to and use today to describe the world around us.

On the other hand, many of these examples also helped foster negative public attitudes about government by lifting up fictional and true stories of corruption and government failure.

So, how can we engage the power of culture to shape hearts and minds in today's cultural and political context?

Several decades ago, before the proliferation of communication channels, TV shows, music and films (both fiction and documentary) tied large numbers of people together in shared experience and common cultural references.

Audience fragmentation makes this much more difficult today but there are promising signs that culture can still play a vital role in contributing to social change. Technology can reach and connect millions of people together. For example, a viral video from the 2017 Women's March of the artist Milck leading a flash mob singing "I Can't Keep Quiet" has made the song into an unofficial anthem of the women's movement.

While every song won't go viral and the production of pop culture may be beyond the reach of the progressive infrastructure, we should constantly be on the lookout for opportunities to partner with musicians, filmmakers, writers, visual artists, and others who are speaking to large audiences. For example, there are a growing number of musicians in virtually every popular genre, from country to hip hop, who write and perform songs about race, war, and justice. They do so for audiences of every size, from stadium crowds to more intimate club gatherings.

We need to make sure that artists, musicians, filmmakers are an integral part of the progressive infrastructure and action to educate, inspire, and knit together a growing community.

There are scores of examples of public policy and public servants who save lives, provide valuable services and knit together communities. For example, Francis Kelsey, an obscure FDA scientist, singlehandedly prevented the dangerous drug Thalidomide from entering the U.S. market. Cultural forms can play a powerful role in lifting up these kinds of stories.

There are also many similar stories of ordinary people taking collective action for the common good both in fiction (i.e. *Harry Potter*) and the world around us (i.e. *Selma.*) There are many more that can and should be lifted up also.

We should also pay attention to the way government is portrayed in popular culture (e.g. *The Andy Griffith Show*, *West Wing*, *Parks and Rec* and *The Mayor*) and among progressive artists about who causes and how government failures happen. And take steps to make the cultural creators aware of how their work can inadvertently support conservative narratives about government and public goods and how they can help advance pro-public values while still lifting up important issues, corruption and government failure.

10. Plant Before Harvesting: Focus on the Work that Gives Meaning to Elections

Progressives of every stripe agree that elections matter. Some have even argued that every progressive organization should make local, state, and federal election campaigns a major focus at key times in every electoral cycle. If we lived under a different tax and funding structure, that might make sense. But we don't.

While elections are the critical piece to gaining governing power, it would be a mistake to concentrate energies on elections to the detriment of the organizing, research, policy campaigns, communications, and leadership development that give elections their meaning and expand the window of the possible after they happen.

As should be clear by now, elections are about harvesting the results of what happens in the time between them: the unfolding of issues that concern voters, the civic actions voters engage in, and the participation of voters in organizations and institutions that keep them connected. The right wing understands this. For example, the Koch Brothers-funded Americans for Prosperity has more than 650 permanent, full-time staff in the states carrying out organizing, trainings, and grassroots lobbying campaigns.

Elections provide concrete outcomes and measurable impacts; in a democracy they are the only way to gain governing power. But they just one part of a comprehensive approach to rebuilding and institutionalizing a commitment to the common good across the country and that will allow elected officials to go further to pass laws and create programs in the public interest.

Conclusion

It is still too early to fully grasp the long-term implications of the Trump presidency. Where it came from is easier to discern: a chaotic mixture and an inevitable result of ideological dominance; the "hardening" of the social-conservative right (focused on abortion, guns, religion) who are willing to ignore the moral and ethical values that would have certainly rejected a man like Trump[68]; the political rise of corporate libertarians like the Koch Brothers; the revolt of the "left out," who blame the wrong forces and people—blacks, immigrants, and government workers—for their real problems; and the political warriors who take no prisoners on the road to victory.

Many progressives believed it was beyond the realm of the possible that Trump could win. But that is also true of many ideological conservatives, for whom character and morality were important parts of their world view. We can only hope they are reflecting on their role in getting us to this point and wondering what to do next.

We should not give in to the temptation of reductionism—that we can find the one idea, strategy or solution instead of striving for an unfettered and sophisticated understanding of changing conditions, contradictions, and crosscurrents. Nor should we reduce progressive ideas and strategies to a narrow or dogmatic ideological, programmatic, or structural agenda and plan.

Conservatives ideologues and progressives both believe they are losing in the age of Trump. At the beginning of George W. Bush's second term, Milton Friedman bemoaned the frustrations of ideological conservatives: "After World War II, opinion was socialist while practice was free market; currently, opinion is free market while practice is heavily socialist"[69]. Today, old line conservatives like Bill Kristol worry that Trump is destroying the conservative movement they've built.

It's important to remember that a significant strain of conservative populist and ideological antigovernment sentiment is equally concerned about corporate power.[70] Even Milton Friedman spoke of his frustration with a "failure to distinguish between being pro-free enterprise and pro-business" that "led persons opposed to a particular business to oppose free enterprise."

> 66 *Over and over again you have the big businessman who talks very effectively about the great virtues of free enterprise and, at the same time, he is off on a plane to Washington to push for special legislation or some special measures for his own benefit."*
>
> **— MILTON FRIEDMAN** [71]

Corporate interests and social conservatives, though, are clearly willing to take advantage of the moment to lower taxes, expand religious exemptions to federal and state laws and reduce public health and safety regulations.

Our task is to organize a pro-public, pro-democracy movement that makes government work for the majority. It should be clear by now that there are no easy answers, no one winning message, no one master plan, and no one organization that can do it alone. But we can start by trying and trying together.

BIBLIOGRAPHY

Much has been written about the rise of conservative movements and the ideological and political assault on the New Deal consensus. Below are some that I have found helpful for understanding strategy and the multiple strands and sectors at play. It is a partial list.

Important Conservative Papers and Articles

1. Screen Guide for Americans, Ayn Rand for The Motion Picture Alliance for the Preservation of American Ideals, 1947

2. The Powell memo commissioned by the U.S. Chamber of Commerce in 1971

3. Stuart Butler (Heritage Foundation and Cato) wrote a series of important strategy papers, including Achieving a "Leninist" Strategy and Privatization: A Strategy to Cut the Budget, that describe privatization as a political strategy to divide pro-budget/pro-government constituencies.

4. William Simon, "Big Government and Our Economic Woes," *Reader's Digest,* 1975

5. *Wall Street Journal* series by Irving Kristol attacking a "new class" who "make their careers in expanding the public sector," 1975

6. Grover Norquist's 2001 article in *The American Spectator*, "The Coming Bush Dynasty: It will flourish if it knocks down key Clinton pillars," laying out a political strategy for permanent political control.

7. Richard Fink, President, Charles G. Koch Charitable Foundation, "The Structure of Social Change," 2012

Important Conservative Books

1. *The Road to Serfdom*, Friedrich Hayek, 1944

2. *Capitalism and Freedom*, Milton Friedman, 1962

3. *Calculus of Consent: Logical Foundations of Constitutional Democracy,* James M. Buchanan and Gordon Tullock, 1962

4. *Privatization Watch*, a Reason Foundation periodical published three times per year since 1976.

5. *A Time for Truth*, William Simon, 1978

6. *The Way the World Works*, Jude Wanniski, 1978

7. *Free to Choose, A Personal Statement,* Milton and Rose Friedman, 1980

8. *Cutting Back City Hall*, Robert Poole, 1980

9. *Wealth and Poverty*, George Gilder, 1981

10. *The New Right: We're Ready to Lead*, Richard Viguerie with forward by Jerry Falwell, 1981

11. *Better Government at Half the Price*, James Bennett, 1981

12. *Privatizing the Public Sector: How to Shrink Government*, E.S. Savas, 1982

13. *Dismantling the State: The Theory and Practice of Privatization*, Madsen Pirie, 1985

14. *Micropolitics*, Madson Pirie, 1988

Important Books Analyzing the Rise of the Right

1. *Ethics and Profits: The Crisis of Confidence in American Business*, Leonard Silk and David Vogel, 1976

2. *Thunder on the Right: The "New Right" and the Politics of Resentment*, Alan Crawford, 1980

3. *Liberalism at Work: The Rise and Fall of OSHA*, Charles Noble, 1986

4. *Fluctuating Fortunes: The Political Power of Business in America*, David Vogel, 1989

5. *Spiritual Warfare, the Politics of the Christian Right*, Sara Diamond, 1989

6. *Shrinking the State: The Political Underpinnings of Privatization*, Harvey Feigenbaum, Jeffrey Henig and Chris Hamnett, 1998

7. *Under Fire: The NRA and the Battle for Gun Control*, Osha Gray Davidson, 1998

8. *The Paradox of American Democracy: Elites, Special Interests and the Betrayal of Public Trust*, John Judis, 2001

9. *Before the Storm: Barry Goldwater and the Unmaking of the American Consensus*, Rick Perlstein, 2001

10. *Upsizing Democracy: Confronting the Right Wing Assault on Government*, Lee Cokorinos, 2007

11. *The Samaritan's Dilemma: Should Government Help Your Neighbor*, Deborah Stone, 2008

12. *The Rise of the Conservative Legal Movement: The Battle for Control of the Law*, Steven M. Teles, 2010

13. *Invisible Hands: The Businessmen's Crusade Against the New Deal*, Kim Phillips-Fein, 2010

14. *Age of Fracture*, Daniel T. Rodgers, 2011.

15. *The Great Persuasion: Reinventing Free Markets since the Depression*, Angus Burgin, 2012

16. *Freedom to Harm: The Lasting Legacy of the Laissez Faire Revival*, Thomas McGarity, 2013

17. *Dog Whistle Politics: How Coded Racial Appeals Have Reinvented Racism and Wrecked the Middle Class*, Ian Haney López, 2015

18. *American Amnesia: How the War on Government Led Us to Forget What Made America Prosper*, Jacob Hacker and Paul Pierson, 2016

19. *Listen Liberal: Or, What Ever Happened to the Party of the People?*, Thomas Frank, 2016

20. *Dark Money: The Hidden History of the Billionaires Behind the Rise of the Radical Right*, Jane Mayer, 2016

21. *The One Percent Solution: How Corporations Are Remaking America One State at a Time*, Gordon Lafer, 2017

22. *Democracy in Chains: The Deep History of the Radical Right's Stealth Plan for America*, Nancy MacLean, 2017

23. *Fear City: New York's Fiscal Crisis and the Rise of Austerity Politics*, Kim Phillips-Fein, 2017

24. *The Color of Law: A Forgotten History of How Our Government Segregated America*, Richard Rothstein, 2017

A Few Progressive Books and Sources

1. *Economics & the Public Purpose*, John Kenneth Galbraith, (1973)

1. *All Together Now: Common Sense for a Fair Economy*, Jared Bernstein (2006)

1. *Whose Freedom*, George Lakoff, (2006)

1. *The Case for Big Government*, Jeff Madrick, (2009)

1. *Why David Sometimes Wins*, Marshall Ganz, (2009)

2. *Culture Change vs. "A Win,"* Topos Partnership Memo (2012)

3. *What Money Can't Buy: The Moral Limits of Markets*, Michael J. Sandel (2012).

4. *Advancing Racial Equity and Transforming Government: A Resource Guide to Put Ideas in Action*, Government Alliance on Race & Equity

5. *Read My Lips: Why Americans Are Proud to Pay Taxes*, Vanessa S. Williams (2017).

Endnotes

1   Sean Wilentz, The Damage Trump Has Done," Rolling Stone, November 30, 2017

2   Charlie Sykes, *How the Right Lost Its Mind*, (New York, St. Martin's Press, 2017)

3   Andrew Rich, "War of Ideas," *Innovation Review,* Spring 2005

4   Michael J. Sandel, "What Isn't for Sale?," *The Atlantic,* April 2012

5   Alexander Hertel-Fernandez and Theda Skocpol, "Five Myths About the Koch Brothers— And Why It Matters to Set Them Straight," *Moyers and Company*, March 10, 2016

6   Pew Research Center, "Public Trust in Government: 1958 – 2017," May 3, 2017

7   Leonard Silk and David Vogel, "*Ethics and Profits: The crisis of confidence in American Business*, (New York: Simon and Shuster, 1976)

8   The *New York Times*, "Excerpts from 'All Together Now: Common Sense for a Fair Economy by Jared Bernstein," July 19, 2006

9   Lee Moran, "GOP Lawmaker Asks Why Men Pay For Maternity Care. Women's Reply is Gold," *HuffingtonPost,* May 16, 2017

10 Despite FDR's philosophical clarity, it's important to recognize that many Americans were excluded from New Deal policies to gain the support of Southern legislators. Those freedoms became the clarion call for the civil rights movement that expanded those policies and rights several decades later.

11 Franklin Delano Roosevelt, Speech to 77th Congress, delivered January 6, 1941

12 Nick Cassella, "Why Republicans Talk About Freedom And Democrats Don't," *Civic Skunk Works,* April 22, 2016

13 Sam Tanenhaus, "The Architect of the Radical Right: How the Nobel Prize-winning economist James M. Buchanan shaped today's antigovernment politics (review of Democracy in Chains by Nancy MacLean,)" *The Atlantic,* July/August 2017

14 Adam Davidson, "Prime Time for Paul Ryan's Guru (the One Who's Not Ayn Rand,)" *New York Times,* August 21, 2012

15 Greg Kaza, "The Mont Pelerin Society's 50th Anniversary: The Society Helps Keep Alight the Lamp of Classical Liberalism," *Foundation for Economic Education,* June 1, 1997

16 William L. Baker, "Book Review: Free to Choose: A Personal Statement by Milton and Rose Friedman," *Foundation for Economic Education,* August 1, 1980

17 Michael Tomasky, "Q & A with Michael Sandel: From Market Economy to Market Society," *The Daily Beast,* July 3, 2012

18 The Powell Memo (also known as the Powell Manifesto), Published August 23, 1971 (Found on *Reclaim Democracy)*

19 Valerie Strauss, "The Koch brothers' influence on college campus is spreading," *Washington Post,* March 28, 2014

20 Caitlin Reilly, "A New Challenge to Koch Gifts on Campus Raises Larger Issues About Transparency," *Inside Philanthropy,* September 25, 2017

21 Deborah Stone, *The Samaritan's Dilemma: Should Government Help Your Neighbor,* (New York: Nation Books, 2008,) 12

22 Dan Baum, "Legalize It All, How to win the war on drugs," *Harpers,* April 2016

23 The Thom Hartmann Program, "The Era of Small Government is Over," *Truthout,* March 10, 2016

24 William Grimes, "Michael Novak, Catholic Scholar Who Championed Capitalism, Dies at 83," *New York Times,* February 19, 2017.

25 Michael Novak, "Who Are The Neoconservatives? A Conversation With Michael Novak," *Crisis Magazine,* March 1, 2007

26 Bill Wilson and Roy Wenzl, "The Koch's quest to save America," *The Wichita Eagle,* October 12, 2012 updated August 13, 2014

27 Richard Viguerie, David Franke, *America's Right Turn, How Conservatives Used New and Alternative Media to Take Power,* (Taylor Trade Publishing, 2004,) 128

28 Joel Achenbach, Scott Higham and Sari Horwitz, "How NRA's true believers converted a marksmanship group into a mighty gun lobby," *Washington Post,* January 12, 2013

29 Jonathan Cohn, "Why Public Employees Are the New Welfare Queens" *New Republic,* August 7, 2010

30 Stuart Butler, "Changing The Political Dynamics of Government," *Proceedings of the Academy of Political Science, Vol. 36, No. 3, Prospects for Privatization,* 1987

31 Report of the President's Commission on Privatization, "Privatization: Toward a More Effective Government," March 1988

32 Nancy Maclean, *Democracy in Chains, The Deep History of the Radical Right's Stealth Plan for America,"* (New York: Viking, 2017,) 144

33 Michael Sean Winters, *Left at the Altar: How the Democrats Lost the Catholics and How the Catholics Can Save the Democrats*, (New York: Basic Books,) 2008

34 Jessica Rettig, "The Religious Ties of the Republican Party," *U.S. News & World Report,* December 2, 2010

35 *Democracy in Chains,* p. 181

36 Stuart Taylor, Jr., "Legal Aid For the Poor: Reagan's Longest Brawl," *New York Times,* June 8, 1984

37 Grover Norquist, "The Coming Bush Dynasty: It will flourish if it knocks down key Clinton pillars," *the American Spectator,* February 2011 (accessed on: https://www.yumpu.com/en/document/view/36469695/the-coming-bush-dynasty-cry-wolf-project)

38 Howell Raines, "Reagan Reversing Many U.S. Policies," *New York Times,* July 3, 1981

39 Jay MacLeod, *Ain't No Makin' It: Aspirations and Attainment in a Low Income Neighborhood,* (New York: Westview Press, 3rd Edition, 2008)

40 Tim Dickinson, "How the GOP Became the Party of the Rich," *Rolling Stone,* November 9, 2011

41 Clara Jeffery and Monica Bauerlein, "The Job Killers: Why are Republicans determined to snuff the recovery," *Mother Jones*, November/December 2011

42 Gordon Lafer, "Corporate power in state legislatures produces a gerrymandered Congress," *Working Economics Blog, Economic Policy Institute,* May 18, 2017

43 Nick Hillman, "Party Control in Congress and State Legislatures (1978 – 2016)," *University of Wisconsin website*

44 Nikole Hannah-Jones, "Have We Lost Sight of the Promise of Public Schools," *New York Times,* February 21, 2017

45 Ian Haney-Lopez and Robert Reich, "The Way Forward for Democrats Is to Address Both Class and Race," *The Nation,* December 12, 2016

46 Peter Dreier, "Most Americans Are Liberal, Even If They Don't Know It," *The American Prospect*, November 10, 2017

47 Gallup News, "Americans Still More Trusting in Local Over State Government," September 19, 2016

48 Chris Cilizza, "There are a remarkably small number of people who trust the government," *Washington Post,* April 21, 2015

49 John Horrigan and Lee Rainie, "Americans' Views on Open Government Data," Pew Research Center, April 21, 2015

50 Center for Transportation Excellence, "2016 Election Results"

51 The Wheeler Report, "School Referendum Results, 2016"

52 Thomas Palley, "A theory of economic policy lock-in and lock-out via hysteresis: rethinking economists' approach to economic policy," Economics, July 4, 2017

53 Mark Binelli, "The Great Kansas Tea Party Disaster," *Rolling Stone*, October, 23, 2014

54 John Kenneth Galbraith, Economics & the Public Purpose, (New York: Signet, 1973,) 215

55 Eugene Kiely, "'You Didn't Build That,' Uncut and Unedited," FactCheck.org, July 24, 2012

56 Jacob Hacker and Paul Pierson, "Don't Dismantle Government — Fix It," The American Prospect, April 1, 2016

57 Lee Fang and Nick Surgey, " Koch Brothers Orchesgtrated Grassroots Effort to Lower Corporate Taxes, Documents Show," The Intercept, Jul 26, 2017

58 Thomas B. Edsall, "Liberals Need to Take Their Fingers Out of Their Ears," *New York Times*, December 7, 2017

59 Angus Burgin, The Great Persuasion: Reinventing Free Markets since the Depression, (Cambridge, MA: Harvard University Press, 2012,) 196 –197

60 Burgin, p. 196 –197

61 Burgin, p. 197

62 Farah Stockman, "Recalling the Nixon-Kennedy health plan," *Boston Globe*, June 23, 2012

63 Richard Viguerie, The New Right: We're Ready to Lead, (Virginia, Viguerie Company, 1981)

64 Indivisible website, https://www.indivisibleguide.com/act-locally/

65 David Leonhardt, "Democrats, Don't Be Fooled By Victory," *The New York Times*, November 12, 2017

66 Mary Gauthier, Americanafest Workshop: Woody Guthrie & Songs for Social Change, September 14, 2017

[67] Ayn Rand, written for The Motion Picture Alliance for the Preservation of American Ideals, 1947

[68] Gary Silverman, "How the Bible Belt lost God and found Trump," *Financial Times*, April 13, 2017

[69] Burgin, p. 223

[70] Guy Molyneux, "A Tale of Two Populisms," *The American Prospect*, June 1, 2017

[71] Burgin, p. 194